Pennsylvania German Fraktur and Printed Broadsides

AMERICAN FOLKLIFE CENTER · THE LIBRARY OF CONGRESS

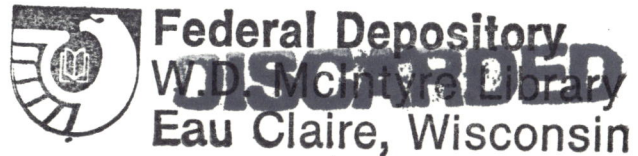

Mein Gott und Vater segne mich;
Der Sohn erhalte gnädiglich
Was er mir hat gegeben.
Der Geist erleuchte Tag und Nacht
Sein Antlitz über mich mit Macht
Und schütze mir mein Leben.
Nur dieses wünsch' ich für und für,
Der Segen Gottes sei mit mir.

Laß Herr dein'n Segen auf mir ruhn,
Mich deine Wege wallen
Und lehre du mich selber thun
Nach deinem Wohlgefallen.
Nimm meines Lebens gnädig wahr;
Auf dich hofft meine Seele;
Sei mir ein Retter in Gefahr
Ein Vater wann ich fehle.

Haus=Segen.

In den drei allerhöchsten Namen,
Vater, Sohn und Heil'ger Geist,
Die das Chor der Engel preißt,
Gesundheit, Ruh' und Segen, Amen.

Gott des Vaters Schöpfers Hand
Segne dieses Haus und Land,
Daß das Futter und die Saaten
Immer mögen wohlgerathen;
Daß der Viehstand wohl gedeihe,
Und sich seines Segens freue.
Daß seine väterliche Güte
Haus und Hof und Stall und Scheuer
Vor Unglück und besonders Feuer
Immer gnädiglich behüte.

Auch geb' er, daß auf jeder Wange
Die edele Gesundheit prange
Und zur Vollendung uns'rer Werke
Geb' er den Gliedern Kraft und Stärke.
Er wende von uns in Gnaden
Hagel= und Gewitter=Schaden.
Auch wolle er die zarten Blüthen
Vor später Kält' und Frost behüten.

Mögen des Erlösers Werke
Ihre Kraft und ihre Stärke
Stets an diesem Haus beweisen;
Daß jedes d'rinn nach Tugend strebe
Und friedlich mit dem andern lebe
Und guten Wandels sich befleiße;
Daß Schand' und Laster insgemein
Entfernt von diesem Hause sein.

Der heil'ge Geist kehr hier auch ein
Und laß' es seine Wohnung sein,
Heil'ge unser Thun und Lassen,
Aus= und Ein=Gang gleichermaßen;
Heil'ge uns zum sel'gen Sterben
Und mach' uns zu Himmels=Erben. — Amen.

Allentaun, [Penns.]
Gedruckt und zu haben bei Gräter und Blumer.

Pennsylvania German Fraktur and Printed Broadsides

A GUIDE TO THE COLLECTIONS IN THE LIBRARY OF CONGRESS

Compiled by

PAUL CONNER & JILL ROBERTS

for the

AMERICAN FOLKLIFE CENTER

Introduction by

DON YODER

Library of Congress · Washington · 1988

Publication of this guide was made possible by the Elizabeth Hamer Kegan Fund, which was established to further the programs and activities of the American Folklife Center.

Cover: Birth certificate for Jacob Meily, b. 1774. (Item Jenks 1.)

Frontispiece: House Blessing. Print, Graeter und Blumer. (Item 130)

Library of Congress Cataloging-in-Publication Data

Library of Congress.
    Pennsylvania German fraktur and printed broadsides.

    (Publications of the American Folklife Center; no. 16)
    Bibliography: p.
    Includes indexes.
    Supt. of Docs. no.: LC 39.8:P38
    1. Fraktur art—Pennsylvania—Pennsylvania Dutch Country—Catalogs. 2. Illumination of books and manuscripts, Pennsylvania Dutch—Catalogs. 3. Pennsylvania Dutch—Folklore—Illustrations—Catalogs. 4. Broadsides—Pennsylvania—Pennsylvania Dutch Country—Catalogs. 5. Library of Congress—Catalogs. I. Connor, Paul. II. Roberts, Jill. III. American Folklife Center. IV. Title. V. Series.
ND3035.P4L48 1988   745.6′7′0893107480740153   88-600044
ISBN 0-8444-0600-7

Publications of the American Folklife Center, No. 16
For sale by the American Folklife Center, Library of Congress, Washington, D.C. 20540

Contents

FOREWORD	7
FRAKTUR: AN INTRODUCTION	9
LIBRARY OF CONGRESS COLLECTIONS	21
Rare Book and Special Collections Division	22
Performing Arts Library	23
Prints and Photographs Division	24
INDEX OF NAMES	44
INDEX OF ARTISTS AND PUBLISHERS	45
SELECTED BIBLIOGRAPHY	46

Foreword

Many magnificent collections are housed in the Library of Congress—books, manuscripts, prints, photographs, recordings, film, and music. One of the most unusual is a significant collection of fraktur and printed broadsides, the folk art of illuminating manuscripts frequently associated with Pennsylvania German communities during the late eighteenth and nineteenth centuries. The Library's collection of hand-painted and printed manuscripts is primarily in the Prints and Photographs Division, with several fine examples in the Rare Book and Special Collections Division and the Performing Arts Library.

Fraktur is of special interest to students of Pennsylvania Dutch (German) folklore and the popularization of this folk art form. We are especially indebted to Don Yoder, professor of folklore and folklife at the University of Pennsylvania for his essay, an introduction to the subject of fraktur. Professor Yoder is a recognized scholar of Pennsylvania German cultures. Our thanks go to Paul Connor, a student of fraktur as an art form, and Jill Roberts, a fine arts specialist with experience in the Prints and Photographs Division, who were engaged by the center to compile a complete list of fraktur in the Library's collections.

The American Folklife Center is pleased to provide this guide to a special collection of American folk art at the Library of Congress.

    Ray Dockstader
    American Folklife Center

Item 153. Print, Moser und Peters, 1826.

Fraktur: An Introduction

Fraktur is a phenomenon in the world of American folk art rooted in the Pennsylvania Dutch (Pennsylvania German) culture. The word *fraktur,* when used for a type of art, is an Americanism. In German, the word means either a particular typeface used by printers or letters made into designs. Based on the Latin *fractura,* a "breaking apart," fraktur suggests that the letters are broken apart and reassembled into designs.

In the world of American collecting and connoisseurship, fraktur as a genre of folk art refers to a folk art drawn, penned, and painted on paper, i.e., *manuscript* folk art. Fraktur centers around a text (usually religious), that is decorated to varying degrees with symbolic designs. In Europe, and also in Pennsylvania, the earlier word for such pieces of art was *Frakturschriften* or "Fraktur Writings." (This term is reflected in the title of the book that I consider to be the best historical introduction to the subject, Donald A. Shelley's 1961 *The Fraktur-Writings or Illuminated Manuscripts of the Pennsylvania Germans.*) *Fraktur* then is short for *Frakturschriften.*

To call fraktur an American phenomenon, one must explain that while its earlier roots lie in the European parent cultures of our Pennsylvania Dutch world, in the arts of Switzerland and the Rhine Valley, it blossomed and developed in new directions in America. Here it came to form an even more basic part of everyday culture. Fraktur documents did exist in Europe, but along with them the Pennsylvania Dutchman's ancestors there were exposed to a much wider range of artistic expression than his descendants in eighteenth- and nineteenth-century America. In Pennsylvania during the early settlement era, fraktur art flowered, at least in part, to fill an artistic vacuum that existed in the everyday world of the Pennsylvania Dutch farmer.

Fraktur flowered in the colonial era when those forefathers of the Pennsylvania Dutch—German-speaking emigrants from the Rhineland and Switzerland—settled together in Pennsylvania over an area exactly the size of Switzerland. Cutting their cultural ties with Europe, they developed an original and creative culture on American soil by applying

Item 53. Birth and baptismal certificate for Catharina Heilman, b. 1777, and blessing.

their traditional crafts and craftsmanship to the problems of the American environment. In this cultural blend, fraktur became the principal genre of art available for viewing by the Pennsylvania Dutch. True, a few well-to-do farmers and townsfolk had their portraits painted and framed prints are mentioned occasionally in inventories of household goods. Painted furniture, tavern signs, and tombstones were also at that time to be looked at as art. But for a century, from the mid-eighteenth to mid-nineteenth century, fraktur remained the form of art closest to the Pennsylvania Dutchman and his family.

What was the subject matter of fraktur? Fraktur was a private art, dealing with the role of the individual in Pennsylvania Dutch society. Anthropologists speak of the "rites of passage," the appropriate rituals that attend those life crises when the individual passes from one group in his closeknit society to another. These folk graduation ceremonies, so to speak, involved birth and baptism; puberty, schooling, and confirmation; courtship and marriage; and death and funeral rites.

Most individuals in Pennsylvania Dutch society passed through all these sacred portals. A few individuals escaped marriage, remaining through life in the role of maiden aunt or bachelor uncle, important elements of the extended family in the massive Pennsylvania farmhouses.

The special fraktur documents associated with each of the above rites of passage are: (1) the Birth and Baptismal Certificate (*Taufschein*), (2) the Calligraphic Model, Reward of Merit, or Lastday Gift of Teacher to Student (*Vorschrift*), (3) the Confirmation Certificate (*Confirmationsschein*), (4) the Wedding Certificate (*Trauschein*), and (5) the Memorial (*Denkmal*). Of these the *taufschein* and the *vorschrift* form the vast bulk of fraktur documentation. Wedding and death certificates are relatively rare. For weddings there was another form of art available: the wedding plate with its humorous inscription. For death and burial there was the decorated tombstone.

A few other genres of fraktur exist, for example the Valentine or True Lover's Knot (forms shared with Anglo-American cultures) and the House Blessing (*Haussegen*). In addition there are also found fraktur ballads and hymns, fraktur Bible records, fraktur mottoes, fraktur alphabet books, and fraktur title or inscription pages of gift books, Bibles, testaments, church records, and manuscript music books used in the singing schools of the Dutchland. All of these examples can be considered fraktur art since they combine the two necessary elements—a text done in fraktur lettering, with designs surrounding or embellishing the text. Occasionally one also finds watercolor or pen pictures which some scholars subsume under the fraktur rubric even though the picture itself dominates the piece and there is very little lettering. These were usually called by their makers not *Frakturschriften* but *Bilder*—"pictures."

Item 3. Margreta Koumin (fl. 1812–1822), artist. Writing example from the New Testament, March 29, 1822.

Who produced fraktur? While it used to be popular to suppose that "folk" art was produced indiscriminately by everyone in a "folk" culture, from toddler to nonagenarian, reason finally demonstrated that, in traditional societies like that of rural Pennsylvania, the "folk" art was produced by specialists. The average Pennsylvania Dutchman did not produce his fraktur baptismal certificate any more than he constructed his house singlehanded, or built his very own Conestoga wagon. Even in its pioneer stages of settlement, every rural community was indeed a community of craftsmen and clients, of producers and consumers, of builders and buyers.

In these country communities, and eventually in the small towns that grew up as trade centers, the individuals whom we dignify with the name "fraktur artists" did indeed produce art for their communities; but their production was a sideline to their major occupations. They were not studio artists producing public art for a wealthy clientele, but individuals who in addition to their major occupation produced private art for private individuals with whom they came in contact in church and school.

The great majority of the artists who produced the thousands of pieces that we admire today were either ministers in the Lutheran and Reformed churches—the majority religions of the Pennsylvania Dutch—or schoolmasters in the parochial schools run by these churches or by the sectarian groups such as the Mennonites, Brethren, and Schwenkfelders. (Curiously enough, the Moravians produced relatively little fraktur. This is probably because Moravianism produced a much broader spectrum of elite art like portraiture and religious paintings, which were part of every Moravian's visual world.) In the exciting game of detective work to identify the now unknown frakturists, the great majority are turning out to be country schoolmasters.

What was the function of fraktur art? In any society from the primitive to the complex, art has multiple functions. Taking the functionalist view of culture, art is only one integral part of a larger cultural whole in which all parts of the culture interact with each other. But an analysis of the art produced by a culture can lead us to an understanding of the meanings, the worldview, the value systems of the society that produced the culture. So the first function of fraktur art is that it records events in the individual's life, as the individual moves through the rites of passage from one social group into the next. These transitions were essentially the four rites of passage introduced earlier: (1) from nameless and unbaptized infant to named and baptized person; (2) from baptized to confirmed membership in the church; (3) from teenage, unmarried, and dependent status to adult, married, and independent status in a new household; and (4) from (as Swiss folklife scholar Richard Weiss put it) the community of the living to the community of the dead. Thus regarded, the documents that recorded these changes of state and status were intensely personal. They were made for and meant for individuals, who treasured them through life. Hence most fraktur art is an art for the individual, i.e., a private rather than a public art.

Secondly, a study of fraktur art enables us to begin to understand the complex belief systems of the Pennsylvania Dutch culture. As most of the texts are religious, they are often the key to central beliefs, clues both to religious faith and the way in which this faith translated into behavior. Again, the individual to whom the piece belonged and for whom it was made could take comfort from reading "his" or "her" texts, throughout life, remembering the gift and the maker, and receiving spiritual encouragement from the words. The texts themselves were part of the Pennsylvania Dutchman's broad repertoire of devotional reading from Bible, hymnal, and prayerbook.

Thirdly, fraktur art was a permitted form of art in cultures that frowned upon public art and public display. The sectarian groups in the Pennsylvania Dutch world—Mennonites, Brethren, Schwenkfelders, Amish, and others—took a negative, essentially puritan view of art. Public art, art for display, was forbidden. Therefore fraktur—private, unobtrusive, and essentially Protestant in its emphasis on religious texts—became a permitted form of art in all the Pennsylvania Dutch groups.

Lastly, fraktur is art. It delights the eye as well as refreshing the spirit. The bright colors, the ingenious combination of text, picture, and overall design, and the curious and now archaic folk symbols are a visual delight whether or not we understand the symbolic and cultural implications behind them. For example, mermaids were often put on baptismal certificates, representing the water spirits in lakes and springs. In Germanic mythology these were believed to deliver newborn babies to the midwives, who then took them back to the waiting mothers. At least this was the story as told to curious Dutch children, just as Anglo-Americans use the stork as symbol of birth. And who can resist those portly Dutch angels blowing trumpets of joy and all those fiddling and dancing figures on a baptismal certificate? They go far to convince us that in the old days the birth and baptism of a child was a real occasion of joy in family and community. There was often in fact a Pennsylvania Dutch baptismal party at which the birth and the newly named child were celebrated.

Item 69. Friederich Krebs (fl. 1780s–1815), artist. Birth and baptismal certificate for Johannes Heinle, b. 1805.

Item 110. Adam und Eva, im Paradies. Print, C. A. Bruckman.

How was fraktur displayed in the traditional Pennsylvania Dutch home? Actually, most of it wasn't. Today we frame and display fraktur pieces on our walls, using them as decoration, museums have "fraktur rooms," but our Pennsylvania Dutch forefathers usually kept their highly individual fraktur pieces, fortunately for us, away from the light, in Bibles or other large books, pasted onto the inside lids of blanket chests, or rolled up in bureau drawers. I will never forget that thrilling moment in my own life—a real rite of passage—when one of my favorite Dutch aunts opened her bureau drawer and presented me with a roll of all my family's fraktur documents from the 1780s to the 1860s. I do not, however, keep them in my bureau drawer. Yielding to current custom, I had most of them framed, and I occasionally display them on walls, walls that do not receive direct sunlight.

Although they often bear some resemblance to fraktur, prints of the Pennsylvania Dutch were something else. They were often framed and put on the walls of homes and taverns, where they functioned as visual art with all its nuances. The upcountry and city presses of the Pennsylvania Dutch culture were busy in the late eighteenth and first half of the nineteenth century producing broadsides and prints.

These two, broadsides and prints, are closely related. A broadside is by definition a sheet of paper printed on one side. This definition could include the print as well, except that we usually divide them by insisting that a broadside features a text and a print features a picture. Broadsides were ephemeral, their purpose was to note passing events. They began in fact as vehicles for spreading news, and long continued as an adjunct to the newspaper. For example, tragedies, local as well as national, were recorded on broadsides, often in the form of a lugubrious ballad that was sung on the streets and in the marketplace, wherever people gathered. People learned the tune from hearing a street singer perform all thirty-two verses of the song, and paid the singer a penny or two for the broadside to remember the words.

There was a significant transfer from the world of manuscript fraktur art to the world of the broadside and the print. Beginning in the eighteenth century, some *taufschein* artists like Heinrich Otto of Lancaster County went to country printers and ordered batches of blank birth and baptismal certificates. These they colored and filled in with the appropriate dates, and added freehand designs as the spirit moved them. As the nineteenth century proceeded, these printed *taufscheins* became more and more numerous. They show a carryover of folk motifs from the older European folk repertoire, but increasingly these are replaced or shoved aside by newer American motifs from the popular culture. These

Item 89. Birth and baptismal certificate for Thomas Monro Zettelmayer, b. 1840.

Item 90. Birth and baptismal certificate for Theyna Chapel, b. 1830.

include the American eagle, the flag, the all-seeing eye, neoclassical urns and altars, and other aspects of national and stylish art. By the 1860s the printed *taufschein* forms had almost completely replaced the manuscript fraktur forms. The printed forms themselves had undergone an esthetic transformation. They went Victorian, so to speak, with shaded romantic figures, wreaths and floral arrangements, and all the accoutrements of rampant Victorianism. This was farewell to fraktur except for certain archaic pockets of fraktur production in Pennsylvania Dutch culture, the best example being the Old Order Amish and the Old Order Mennonites. Both of these ultra-conservative groups continued into the twentieth century to decorate bookplates and inscribe fraktur family registers into their Bibles and other devotional books.

The symbolic prints of the Pennsylvania Dutch are an important American example of the continuance on American soil of European folk and popular print motifs. Many of these prints that issued from the country presses and appeared on the walls of Pennsylvania farmhouses and taverns were based on European originals, making comparative studies of European prototypes a necessity. This is not to say that the American copies remained completely derivative. In the hands of clever engravers the European original took on definite American character.

One of the most talented publishers of broadsides and prints in all of America was the Harrisburg printer Gustavus Sigismund Peters (1793–1847). An emigrant from Saxony, Peters had in the 1820s set up a press in Carlisle, Pennsylvania, whence he removed to Harrisburg, the state capital. His production was bilingual, German and English, and catered to the religious, occult, and secular tastes of the Pennsylvania Dutch clientele. From 1825 until his death he issued thousands of German books, pamphlets, chapbooks, broadsides, printed fraktur pieces, children's toy books, and especially, allegorical and religious prints. For these he did his own engraving and his woodcuts are superb.

Among his prints there are two that deserve detailed mention. The first is "Das Leben und Alter der Menschen," (Item 153.) which shows the progress of human life from birth to death, from the cradle to the grave. The aging process is seen in the conservatizing of dress and the giving up of luxuries. The symbolic animal figures that represent the different ages are significant. The religious verses that accompany the stages and the entire format appealed to the religious mind, hence such art as this could appropriately be framed for display upon the walls of the homes of religiously oriented farmers and craftsmen. The entire piece is a sophisticated "memento mori" such as was popular in many forms in the Victorian era.

Somewhat more weighted toward traditional theology with its rewards and punishments is the graphic "Two Ways" print by Peters. This shows the "broad way that leadeth to destruction" (Matthew 7)— and how graphic it is with its gaping cavern of hell flaming with eternal fires of retribution. Rising above it is the "narrow way that leadeth unto life." Like many manuscript fraktur pieces, this print is oriented with an earth side and a heaven side, the heaven side in this case being the "New Jerusalem," the spiritual heaven from the book of Revelation. Traditional symbols, sun, moon, and stars also continue to adorn this piece. In a sense the Two Ways is a drawing of the spiritual universe, portraying the ancient dualism between Satan and Christ, Heaven and Hell, with struggling man caught in the realm of choice between them. It was immensely popular and went through many editions, offered for sale by Peters as well as other early Pennsylvania Dutch printers.

There is one final question that we wish to ask. Are there no parallels to fraktur art in other American cultures? If we use my term *manuscript art* rather than the uniquely Pennsylvania Dutch term *fraktur,* the answer is yes. Fraktur is uniquely Pennsylvania Dutch, but manuscript art did develop in certain other early American ethnic and sectarian groups. The New England Puritans and other Anglo-

Americans including the Quakers indulged in manuscript art, mostly decorated family registers, a permitted form of art in those cultures. Shaker art is another example. In the great spiritual awakening that rocked the Shaker world in mid-nineteenth century, manuscript art was produced in abundance using Shaker symbolism in what have been called both "spirit drawings" and "gift drawings." A third and last example out of others that could be cited is the art of the Russian-German Mennonites who brought their mostly Holland Dutch and Low German cultural traditions from the steppes to the Great Plains in the 1870s. Their art which has recently been analyzed is more closely related to fraktur and involves what the Russian-Germans called *Zierschriften* or "ornamental writings."

In conclusion, the fraktur art of the Pennsylvania Dutch, has, since its discovery by the outside world in the late nineteenth century, taken its place as a central genre of American folk art. In the process it has become the most sought after of all forms of Pennsylvania Dutch artistic production. Collections are housed in major libraries and museums across the nation, and private collectors have assembled equally significant holdings.

Don Yoder
University of Pennsylvania
October 1986

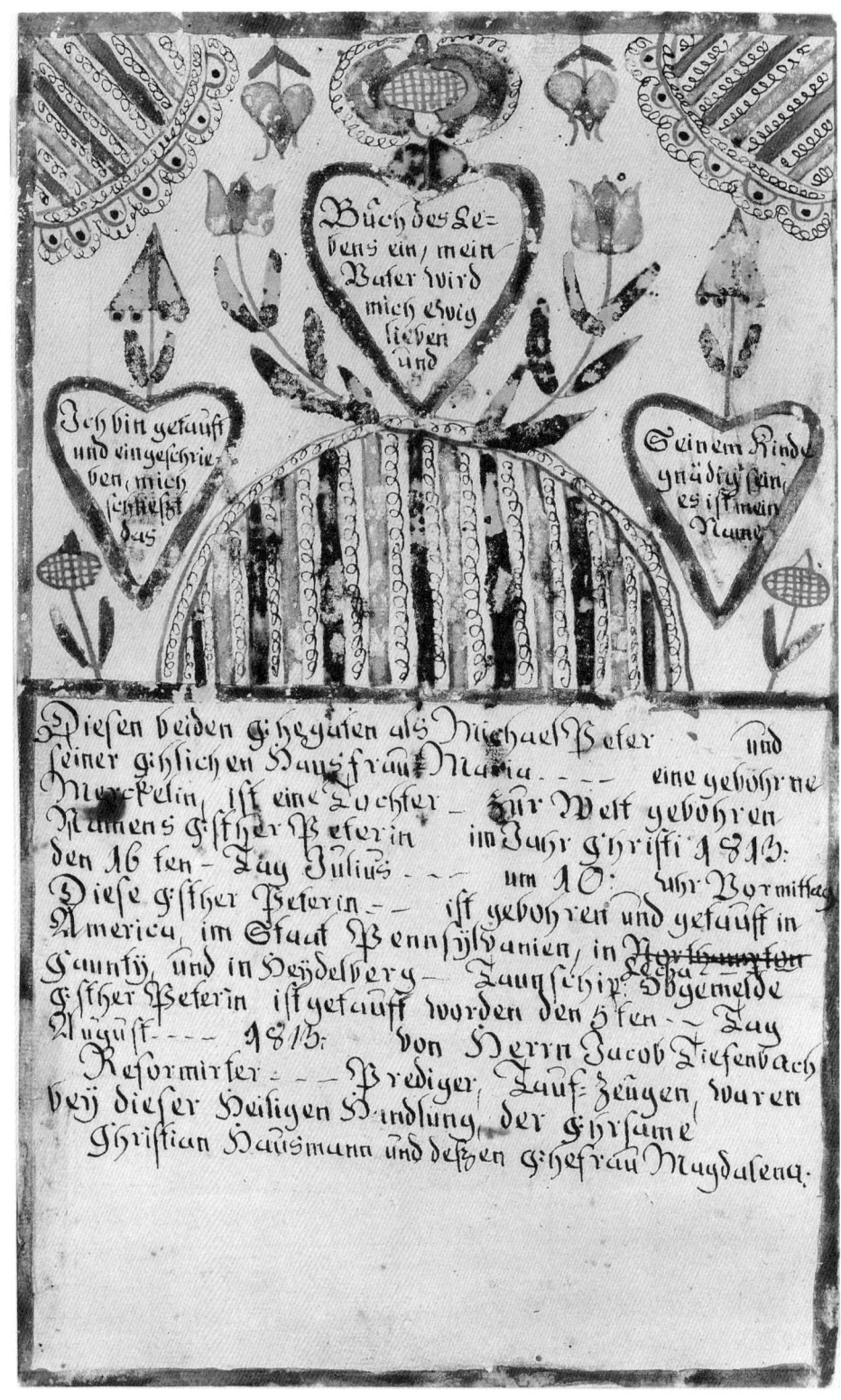

Item 1. Birth and baptismal certificate for Esther Peter, b. 1813.

Library of Congress Collections

Located in the Prints and Photographs, Rare Book and Special Collections, and Music divisions of the Library of Congress is a treasure trove of more than 120 manuscript and printed fraktur and broadsides—decorated folk art on paper associated with the Pennsylvania Dutch, using the old style block lettering.

In 1923 Mrs. Anna Louise Jenks, a government clerk from Landover, Prince Georges County, Maryland, gave six frakturs to the Library of Congress. The gift included one birth certificate decorated by Johannes Schopp, two hymns of Johann Franck, lettered by Henrich Rassmann, and two manuscript epistles of St. Paul and one Wisdom of Sirach verse, decorated in Lancaster County, Pennsylvania. Several dozen more were included in a collection of Pennsylvania German and other American primitive prints and drawings, acquired from Karl Goedecke of Hazleton, Pennsylvania, in 1943.

In the years following the Jenks gift, the Library has acquired many broadsides printed in German, with woodcut illustrations of the Ages of Man, Adam and Eve, selfishness vs. generosity, letters from God, and folksongs. The collection of illuminated manuscripts includes vows of celibacy at the Ephrata Cloister in Lancaster County and the popular birth and baptismal certificates "finished" by Friederich Krebs, with wide-eyed parrots and swelling turnip-shaped hearts.

Well-known fraktur artists represented include Friederich Krebs, Martin Brechall, and Durs Rudy. The printed works came from Allentown, Reading, Philadelphia, Harrisburg, and Lancaster, all in the state of Pennsylvania.

The manuscripts and prints reflect the religious interest of the Lutheran, Reformed, Schwenkfelder, and Anabaptist communities. The frakturs and broadsides demonstrate a skill in calligraphy, appreciation of hymnody, poetry, and humor. This documentation from Pennsylvania Dutch communities reveals a good deal about their religious beliefs, lifestyles, and decorative arts from the mid-1700s to the early 1900s.

Rare Book and Special Collections Division

Although most items in the Library of Congress fraktur collections are located in the Prints and Photographs Division, a few can be found elsewhere. Two are included in books that are housed in the Rare Book and Special Collections Division.

Brant, Samuel.
(Ownership inscription detached from Samuel Brant's copy of the New Testament) 1779.
Spine title on book-shaped slip case: *Pennsylvania Dutch Fraktur Work*. March 17, 1779.
Facing pages.
Bookplate, manuscript, (1779); 17.4 × 21.3 cm.
n.p.
Rosenwald Collection, Z 276 .09

Egelmann, Carl Friederich, 1782–1860.
Deutsche & Englische Vorschriften fur die Jugend.
16 leaves.
(Reading: s. n., 1821).
Book, (1821), engravings, 15.5 × 20.4 cm.
Rare Book Collection, LB 1139 .W7 E 36

Performing Arts Library

Among the rare books in the Performing Arts Library are four illuminated manuscripts. The music notation and hymns in German were hand lettered in fraktur in colonial times, from 1746 to 1772. The four books are a product of southeastern Pennsylvania, Lancaster County, of the Ephrata Cloister.

Housed in great Germanic wooden buildings, the commune included sisters and brothers. The Anabaptist community included skilled calligraphers, illuminators, and hymnists. Foremost among the hymn writers was the founder, a Pietist mystic, Johann Conrad Beissel, 1690–1768. His name in religion was Vater Friedsam. Beissel composed much of the music.

The hymn texts and tunes are the earliest original music composed in the British colonies.

Microfilm copies of the manuscripts are in the Performing Arts Library. Printed copies of the tunes and texts were printed at the cloister in the printery of the brotherhood. Copies are in the Rare Book and Special Collections Division.

Ephrata Community: Ephrata Codex.
Die bittre gute, oder das gesaeng der einsamen turtel-taube, der christlichen kirche hier auf erden, die annoch im trauerthal auf den duerren aesten und zweigen den stand ihrer wittenschafft beklaget, und dabey in hoffnung singet von einer andern und nochmaligen vermaehlung.
Johann Conrad Beissel, 1690–1768, composer.
Manuscript: ink and watercolor; 19 × 24.5 cm.
Ephrata, Pa. : 1746.
M 2116 .E6 1746 Case

Ephrata Community.
Music for the hymns in Turtel Taube.
Johann Conrad Beissel, 1690–1768, composer.
Manuscript: ink and watercolor; 17.8 × 21.3 cm.
Ephrata, Pa. : 1747?
Printed index.
Mittel-Buch.
M 2116 .E6 1747(B) Case

Paradisisches wunder-spiel welches sich in diesen letzten zeiten und tagen in denen abendlaendischen welt-theilen als ein vorspiel der neuen welt hervorgethan. Bestehende in einer gantz neuen und ungemeine sing-art auf weise der englischen und himmlischen choere eingerichtet, da dann das lied Mosis und des Lamma wie auch das Hohe Lied Salomons mit samt noch mehrern zeugnussen aus der Bibel und andern heiligen. Wobeÿ dann nicht weniger den zuruf der braut des Lamms samt der zubereitung auf den herrlichen hoch-zeit tag trefflich praefiguriret wird. Alles nach englischen choeren gesangs weise mit viel muehe und grossem fleiss ausgefertiget durch einen Friedsamen der sonst in dieser welt weder namen noch titul suchet.
Johann Conrad Beissel, 1690–1768, composer.
Manuscript: ink and watercolor; 25.1 × 20.2 cm.
Ephrata, Pa.: 1751.
M 2116 .E6 1751 Case

Ephrata Community.
Music book of the Ephrata Cloister.
Johann Conrad Beissel, 1690–1768, composer.
Manuscript: ink and watercolor; 20.7 × 17.1 cm.
Ephrata, Pa.: 1772.
Printed register.
Music to hymns in "Neu vermehrte Turtel Taube."
M 2116 .E6 1772 Case

Prints and Photographs Division

Compilers notes: Measurements were rounded off to the nearest half centimeter due to the extreme unevenness of the paper size of most drawings. Most of the certificates were inscribed with pen and brown ink. The first six items are from the Anna Louise Jenks Collection of Fraktur. An LC number indicates that the fraktur has been photographed and that a negative exists. Copy prints may be ordered from the Library's Photoduplication Service.

LOT 10257 JENKS COLLECTION

1. Birth certificate: Jacob Meily.
   Unidentified artist.
   ca. 1774.
   Pen and brown ink over pencil, with watercolor, on laid paper; 20.5 × 25.5 cm (sheet).

2. Vorschrift.
   Signed: Johannes Meylen gehoret diese Vorshrifft.
   1752.
   Pen and ink and watercolor on laid paper;
      33 × 41 cm (sheet).

3. Vorschrift.
   Signed: Johannes Meylen . . . 1751.
   Pen and ink and watercolor, on laid paper;
      20.5 × 33 cm (sheet).

4. Vorschrift.
   Henrich Rassmann.
   1709.
   Pen and ink, gouache and watercolor, on laid paper; 34 × 41 cm (sheet).

5. Vorschrift.
   Signed: Henrich Rassmann.
   ca. 1709.
   Pen and ink, gouache and watercolor, on laid paper; 20.5 × 34 cm (sheet).

6. Vorschrift.
   Henrich Rassmann.
   ca. 1709.
   Pen and ink, gouache and watercolor, on laid paper; 33.5 × 40 cm (sheet).

LOT 12683

1. Taufschein: Esther Peter.
   Unidentified artist.
   ca. 1813.
   Pen and brown ink and watercolor, on laid paper;
   33.5 × 20.5 cm (sheet).
   LC-USZ62-93921

2. Vorschrift.
   Unidentified artist.
   Pen and brown ink and watercolor, on laid paper;
   20 × 16 cm (sheet).
   Writing sample from New Testament. Epistles.
   Corinthians 1st 1:1–7.
   LC-USZ62-93920

3. Vorschrift.
   Signed: Margreta Koumin, 1822.
   Pen and ink and watercolor, on wove paper;
   19 × 32 cm (sheet).

   Writing sample from New Testament; Epistles,
   Hebrews 9: 11–12.
   LC-USZ62-93922
   LC-USZC4-1217

4. Adam and Eve in Paradise.
   Unidentified artist.
   Pen and ink and watercolor, on wove paper;
   17.5 × 26.5 cm (sheet).

5. The Temptation of Eve.
   Unidentified artist.
   Watercolor and gouache, with scraping out,
   on laid paper; 23.5 × 17.5 cm (sheet).

6. Die Geburt Christi. [The Birth of Christ]
   Imprint: Gedruckt und zu haben bey G. S. Peters.
   Harrisburg, Pa.
   Woodcut with stencil coloring and letterpress,
   on wove paper; 35.5 × 24.5 cm (sheet).

   See entry 118 for duplicate print.

7. Der Einzug Christi in Jerusalem. [The Entry of
   Christ into Jerusalem]
   Woodcut with letterpress and watercolor, on laid
   paper; 19.5 × 25.5 cm (sheet).

   Probably published by G. S. Peters,
   Harrisburg, Pa.
   Compare with entry 119.

8. Bookplate: Catharina Kinnig.
   Unidentified artist (see note).
   1898.
   Pen and ink and watercolor, on laid paper;
   17 × 9.5 cm (sheet).

   Bookplate inscribed "Dieses Buch Gehoret Mir
   Catharina Kinnig Im Jahr 1898." [This book
   plate was made for Catharina Kinnig in the year
   1898.] Kinnig might have made this bookplate
   for herself.
   LC-USZ62-93916

9. Vorschrift: Fraktur Alphabet G–L [on verso]
   and M–Q.
   Signed: Samuel Kundig, 1828.
   Brown ink and watercolor, on wove paper;
   32 × 20 cm (sheet).

   Illegible inscription in lower, left-hand corner.

10. Tulip growing from heart.
    Unidentified artist.
    Pen and ink over pencil, with watercolor, on wove
    paper; 19 × 12 cm (sheet).

11. Valentine: "From a Friend"
    Unidentified artist.
    Brown ink and pencil, with watercolor, on lined,
    wove paper; 31.5 × 20 cm (sheet).

    Verse continues:
      Round is the ring
      that has no end
      So is my love
      For you, my friend.

12. Owl from rear.
    Unidentified artist.
    ca. 1862.
    Watercolor and gouache over pencil, on lined,
    wove paper; 5.5 × 7 cm (sheet).

    Handwriting on verso.

13. Flower in star shape.
    Unidentified artist.
    Pencil and watercolor, on wove paper;
    8 × 9.5 cm (sheet).

14. Three sketches including tulips.
    Signed: J.D.B.
    Pen and brown ink, on wove paper;
    10 × 9 cm (sheet).

    Arithmetic problems on verso.

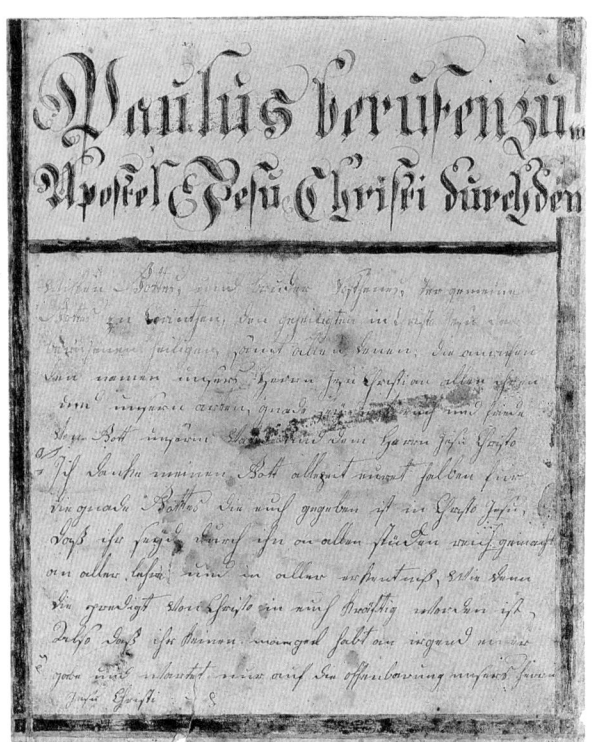

Item 2. Writing example from the New Testament.

Item 8. Bookplate, 1898.

15. Roses.
    Unidentified artist.
    Pen and ink, on wove paper;
    12.5 × 10.5 cm (sheet).

16. Eagle with banner reading "E Pluribis Unum 1852."
    Unidentified artist.
    1852.
    India ink, on blue, wove paper;
    11.5 × 18 cm (sheet).

17. Bird facing right.
    Unidentified artist.
    Pen and brown ink, on lined, wove paper;
    10.5 × 7 cm (sheet).

18. Parrot perched on branch, facing left.
    Unidentified artist.
    Pen and ink wash, on wove paper;
    11 × 8.5 cm (sheet).

    Illegible handwriting on verso.

19. Bird perched on sprig, facing right.
    Unidentified artist.
    Watercolor over pencil, on coated, wove paper;
    9.5 × 9.5 cm (sheet).

20. Bird perched on flowering stem, facing left.
    Unidentified artist.
    Pen and brown ink, on lined, wove paper;
    10 × 10 cm (sheet).

21. Eagle with wings spread.
    Unidentified artist.
    Watercolor over pencil, on laid paper;
    7.5 × 11 cm (sheet).

22. Multicolored eagle with wings spread.
    Unidentified artist.
    Watercolor over pencil, on laid paper;
    7 × 11 cm (sheet).

23. Valentine: "St. Valentine the good of old . . ."
    Unidentified artist.
    1841.
    Watercolor over pencil, with pen and ink, on lined, blue wove paper; 31.5 × 20 cm (sheet).

    Verse continues:
    On this day bids young hearts be bold
    And unto loves sweet voice incline.
    Let us obey St Valentine.

    This is followed by eight more lines of verse.

24. Three story yellow house with shutters, set between two trees.
    Signed: Made by Mrs. Sarah Gregg.
    Watercolor over pencil, on laid paper;
    17 × 20.5 cm (sheet).

    Handwriting on verso.

25. Two story red brick house, set between weeping willow trees.
    Unidentified artist.
    Watercolor over pencil, on wove paper;
    24.5 × 20 cm (sheet).

26. Dauphin County Prison, view taken from Arnets Hotel, called State Capitol.
    Signed: William Rank, August 19, 1850.
    Pencil, pen and ink with watercolor, on wove paper; 18.5 × 28 cm (sheet).

    Dauphin County Prison is located in Harrisburg, Pa.

27. View of farm with rail fences and log barn.
    Signed: W [illiam] Rank.
    Pen and ink and watercolor over pencil, on wove paper; 18.5 × 28 cm (sheet).

    A pencil inscription below image might have been intended as a title but can only be partially decifered. (Possibly "Bean and Smyeths")

28. Log and brick house with fence and weeping willow.
    Unidentified artist.
    Pencil on wove paper; 18.5 × 22 cm (sheet).

29. Decorative floral wreath with nosegay, birds, and insect.
    Unidentified artist.
    Gouache over pencil, on wove paper;
    17.5 × 23 cm (sheet).

30. Assorted flowers in planter.
    Unidentified artist.
    Pen and brown ink, on wove paper;
    23.5 × 18.5 cm (sheet).

31. Pink rose.
    Unidentified artist.
    ca. 1818.
    Stencil, watercolor and brown ink, with overlay, on laid paper; 12.5 × 10 cm (sheet).

    Drawing bears inscription: "Received March 25th, 1818."

32. Single rose in frame.
    Unidentified artist.
    Pen and brown ink with watercolor, on wove paper; 12 × 17.5 cm (sheet).

33. Pedestled font with flowers.
    Signed: Painted by Miss Ruth Whitemore of Windsor New York aged nine years.
    Pen and brown ink and watercolor, with overlays, on wove paper; 22.5 × 18 cm (sheet).

    Poem "by Matilda Whitemore" appears below image.
    LC-USZ62-35578

34. Sprig of pink rosebuds and yellow roses.
    Unidentified artist (see note).
    Watercolor over pencil, on wove paper; 24.5 × 19.5 cm (sheet).

    Probably by same artist as entries 35 and 36.

35. Spray of pink roses in slender, yellow vase.
    Unidentified artist (see note).
    Watercolor over pencil, on wove paper; 24.5 × 20 cm (sheet).

    Probably by same artist as entries 34 and 36.

36. Spray of pink roses.
    Unidentified artist (see note).
    Watercolor over pencil, on wove paper; 24.5 × 20 cm (sheet).

    Probably by same artist as entries 34 and 35.

37. Branch of blossoming flowers.
    Unidentified artist.
    Grey wash and watercolor over pencil, on wove paper; 20 × 10 cm (sheet).

    Corners of paper were rounded off causing measurements to vary greatly.

38. Floral arrangement in yellow wicker basket.
    Unidentified artist.
    Pencil and watercolor, on wove paper; 20 × 13.5 cm (sheet).

39. Black horse and large, yellow dog.
    Unidentified artist.
    Watercolor on lined, wove paper; 5 × 10.5 cm (sheet).

40. Spotted dog leaping into water.
    Signed: A. J. D.
    Black ink and watercolor, over pencil, on wove paper; 13.5 × 14.5 cm (sheet).

41. The Stag.
    Signed: R. A. Dell, 1802.
    Pencil, pen and ink and watercolor, on wove paper; 18 × 11 cm (sheet).

42. Birds perched on river bank.
    Unidentified artist.
    Black wash and watercolor, over pencil, on blue, wove paper; 20.5 × 17 cm (sheet).

43. Four sketches: Pennsylvania German family, jester, soldier on horseback blowing horn; eagle's head.
    Signed: A. J. D.
    Pencil on wove paper; 30 × 20.5 cm (sheet).

44. Come saints and sinners . . .
    Signed: Sarah Wiegner, 1863.
    Pen and brown ink and watercolor, on lined, wove paper; 26 × 26 cm (sheet).

    Poem continues for several verses.
    LC-USZ62-35577

45. Page from arithmetic lesson book.
    Signed: Penrose Wright, 1826.
    Pencil, pen and ink, and watercolor, with overlay, on wove paper; 33.5 × 20 cm (sheet).

    Page from Wright's arithmetic lesson book, having to do with square roots. Handwriting on front and verso.

46. Taufschein: Marriage Record of William Blunt and Mary Furnald. September 12, 1786.
    Signed: Wm. Blunt, 1786.
    Black ink, watercolor, gold leaf, on laid paper, with paper cut silhouettes; 26 × 24 cm (sheet).

    Paper is heart-shaped; measurements taken from center.

47. Man and woman strolling beneath willow tree.
    Unidentified artist.
    Pen and brown ink with watercolor, on laid paper; 13.5 × 18 cm (sheet).

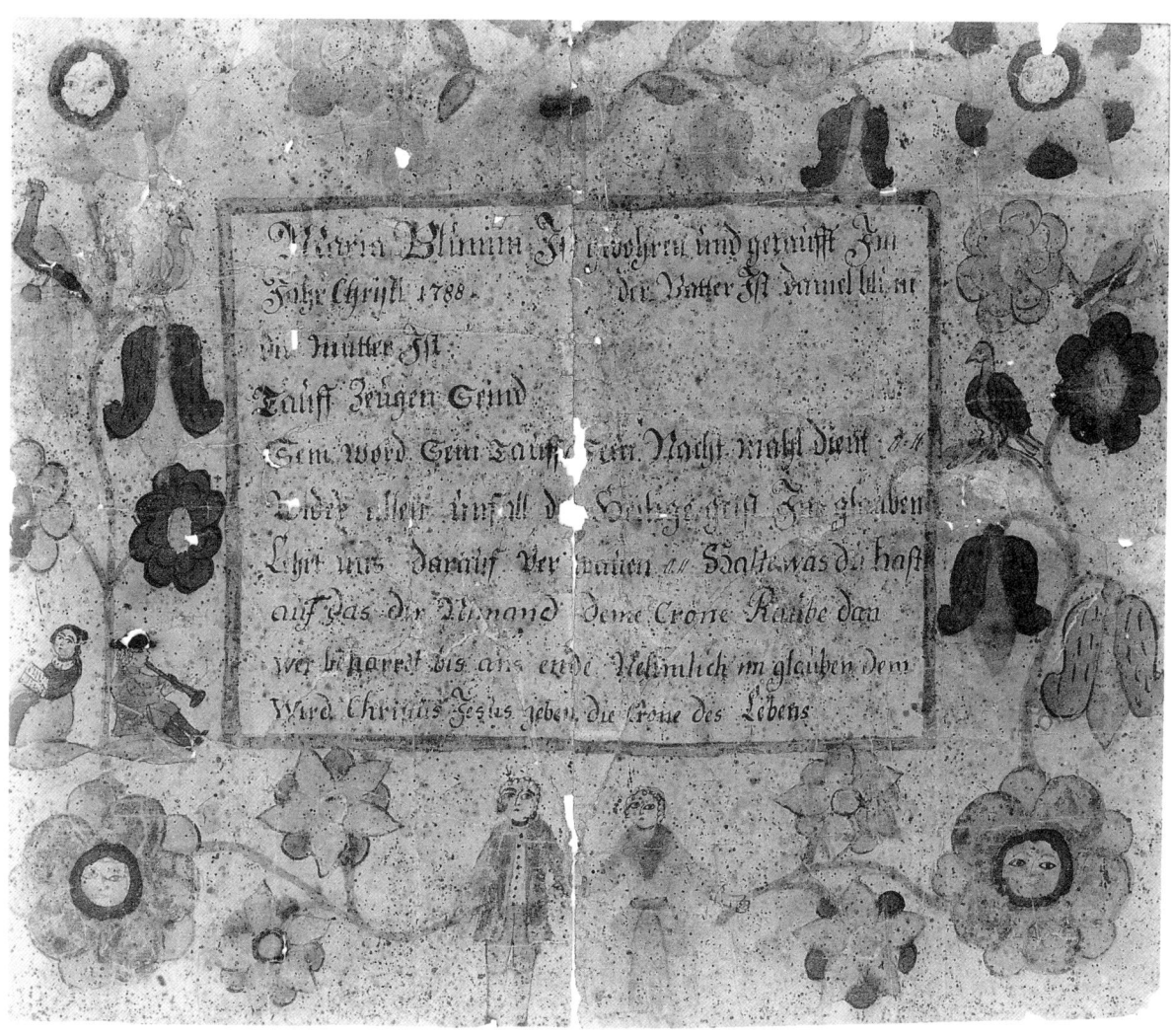

Item 57. Birth and baptismal certificate for Maria Blümin, b. 1788.

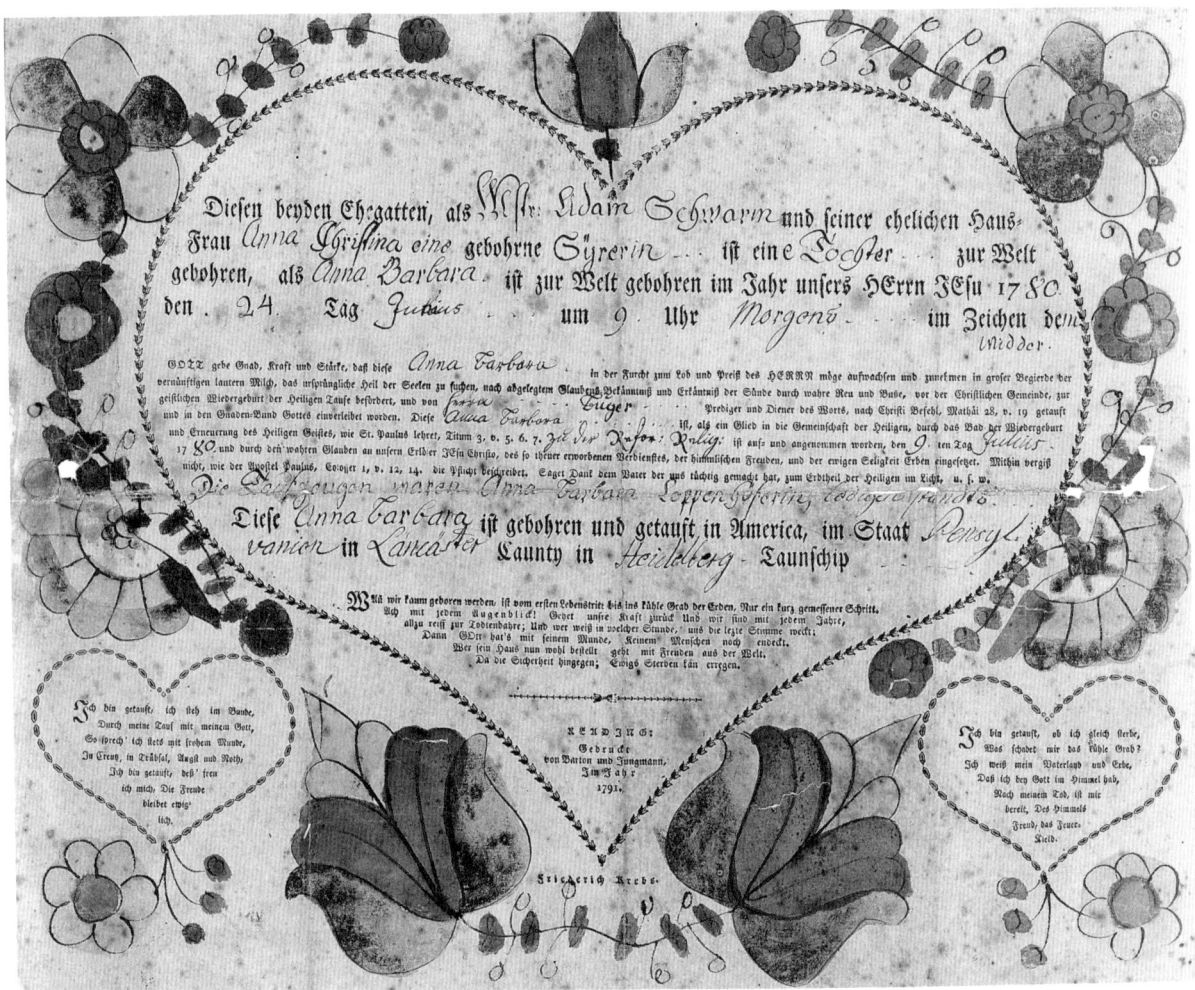

Item 60. Friederich Krebs (fl. 1780s–1815), artist. Birth and baptismal certificate for Anna Barbara Schwarin, b. 1780.

48. Die Apostel Emfangen den Heiligen Geist.
    [The Apostles Receive the Holy Ghost]
    Unidentified artist.
    Engraving, with watercolor, on laid paper;
    27.5 × 20.5 cm (sheet).

49. View of island with tall trees.
    Unidentified artist.
    Watercolor on parchment; 14.5 × 13.5 cm (sheet).

    Image is very faded, making it difficult to distinguish subject of drawing.

50. Man in flowing classical robe, seated between two classical columns with shovel and pick axe.
    Unidentified artist.
    Pen and ink and wash, on laid paper;
    13.5 × 17.5 cm (sheet).

51. Buxom woman wearing large, feathered hat and carrying small chest.
    Unidentified artist.
    Etching with watercolor, on wove paper;
    15.5 × 11 cm (sheet).

    Artist was probably trying to copy style of British artist Thomas Rowlandson.

30

52. Side view of woman in long dress, holding tulip.
    Signed: W. Rieshe.
    ca. 1850.
    Pencil on lined, wove paper; 20 × 15 cm (sheet).

    Inscribed in different handwriting below image: "Lead pencil drawing of 1850."

53. Taufschein: Catharina Heilman.
    Unidentified artist.
    ca. 1777.
    Woodcut with letterpress, watercolor, and pen and ink, on laid paper; 33 × 41 cm (sheet).
    LC-USZ62-93917
    LC-USZC4-1216

54. Taufschein: Jacob Schall.
    Signed: Martin Brechall.
    1803.
    Pen and brown ink and watercolor, on laid paper; 33 × 41 cm (sheet).

55. Taufschein: Magdalena Blossin.
    Unidentified artist.
    1813.
    Pen and ink and watercolor, on laid paper; 27.5 × 42 cm (sheet).

56. Taufschein: Sussanna Blumin.
    Unidentified artist.
    1785.
    Ink and watercolor, on laid paper; 32.5 × 39 cm (sheet).

57. Taufschein: Maria Blümin.
    Unidentified artist.
    ca. 1788.
    Wash, pen and ink, and watercolor, on laid paper; 32 × 38 cm (sheet).
    LC-USZ62-93929

58. Taufschein: Johan Wendel Shadt.
    Imprint: Gedruckt und zu haben bey Wilhelm Lepper, zu Hannover.
    1821.
    Woodcut with letterpress, on laid paper; 32 × 41 cm (sheet).
    LC-USZ62-3141

59. Taufschein.
    Imprint: Libanon: Gedruckt bey J. Stover.
    Woodcut with letterpress, on laid paper; 22 × 40.5 cm (sheet).

    Blank certificate.

60. Taufschein: Anna Barbara Schwarin.
    Signed: Friederich Krebs.
    Imprint: Reading: Gedruckt von Barton und Jungmann, Im Jahr 1791.
    Woodcut with letterpress, pen and brown ink and watercolor, on laid paper; 31.5 × 40 cm (sheet).
    LC-USZ62-93910

61. Taufschein: Sally Neu.
    Imprint: Herausgegeben und zu haben bei Georg W. Menz. No. 71, in der Rehs-Strasse.
    1814.
    Engraving with watercolor, on wove paper; 46 × 36 cm (sheet).

62. Taufschein: Wilhelm Staut.
    Unidentified artist.
    1807.
    Woodcut with watercolor and letterpress, on laid paper; 31.5 × 39.5 cm (sheet).
    LC-USZ62-3138

63. Taufschein: Jacob Rudy.
    Imprint: Ephrata: gedruckt bey Samuel Baumann.
    1812.
    Woodcut with letterpress and watercolor, on laid paper; 31.5 × 38.5 cm (sheet).

64. Taufschein: Jacob Adam.
    Imprint: Reading, Gedruckt von Gottlob Jungmann Im Jahr 1804.
    Woodcut with letterpress and watercolor, on laid paper; 33.5 × 39 cm (sheet).

65. Taufschein: Magdalena Kraemer.
    Imprint: Befertigt von F. Krebs Gedruckt im Jahr 1804.
    Woodcut with letterpress, watercolor, and embossed overlays, on laid paper; 32.5 × 40.5 cm (sheet).

66. Taufschein: Samuel Schwartz.
    Imprint: Befertigt von F. Krebs.
    1808.
    Woodcut with letterpress, watercolor, and embossed overlay, on laid paper; 32 × 39 cm (sheet).

Item 70. Johann S. Wiestling (1787–1842), printer. Birth and baptismal certificate for Johannes Purman, b. 1807.

Item 88. Birth and baptismal certificate for Daniel Gottschall, b. 1813.

67. Taufschein: Henrich Stein.
    Imprint: Befertigt von F. Krebs.
    1808.
    Woodcut with letterpress, watercolor, and pen and brown ink, on laid paper; 32 × 40.5 cm (sheet).

68. Taufschein: Georg Henrich.
    Imprint: Befertigt von F. Krebs.
    ca. 1804.
    Woodcut with letterpress and watercolor, on laid paper; 33 × 40 cm (sheet).

69. Taufschein: Johannes Heinle.
    Imprint: Befertigt von F. Krebs.
    ca. 1806.
    Woodcut with pen and ink, letterpress and watercolor, on laid paper; 32 × 40 cm (sheet).
    LC-USZ62-93915
    LC-USZC4-1215

70. Taufschein: Johannes Purman.
    Imprint: Harrisburg, Gedruckt bey John S. Wiestling.
    ca. 1807.
    Woodcut with letterpress and watercolor on laid paper; 40 × 32 cm (sheet).
    LC-USZ62-93912

71. Taufschein: Peter Keller.
    Imprint: Reading, Gedruckt und zu haben bey Johann Ritter.
    1825.
    Woodcut with letterpress, on wove paper; 41.5 × 33 cm (sheet).

72. Taufschein: Enoch Miller.
    Imprint: Reading, Gedruckt und zu haben bey Johann Ritter.
    ca. 1815.
    Woodcut with letterpress, on wove paper; 40.5 × 32 cm (sheet).

73. Taufschein: Sara Felix.
    Imprint: Gedruckt und zu haben bey Johann Ritter und Companie.
    ca. 1810.
    Woodcut with letterpress and watercolor, on laid paper; 42 × 33 cm (sheet).

74. Taufschein: Leonhardt Rothermel.
    Imprint: Reading, Gedruckt und zu haben bey Johann Ritter und Comp.
    1831.
    Woodcut with letterpress and watercolor, on laid paper; 41.5 × 33 cm (sheet).

75. Taufschein: Salome Wenrich.
    Imprint: Reading, Gedruckt und zu haben bey Johann Ritter und Comp.
    1820.
    Woodcut with letterpress, on wove paper; 41 × 32.5 cm (sheet).

76. Taufschein: Susanna Noll.
    ca. 1797.
    Imprint: Reading, Gedruckt und zu haben bey Johann Ritter und comp.
    Woodcut with letterpress and watercolor, on laid paper; 41 × 34 cm (sheet).

77. Taufschein: Maria Magdalena Stiely.
    Imprint: Reading, Gedruckt und zu haben bey Johann Ritter und Comp.
    between 1802 and 1834.
    Woodcut with letterpress and watercolor, on wove paper; 41.5 × 33 cm (sheet).

    The dating of this print is based on an inscription which notes that Maria Stiely died in 1834. The certificate might have been produced at her birth in 1802 but more likely upon her death in 1834, as a remembrance of her life.

78. Taufschein: Semiel Hermann Steiger.
    Imprint: Reading, Pa, Gedruckt und zu haben bey Ritter u. co.
    ca. 1867.
    Lithograph with watercolor, on wove paper; 43 × 35 cm (sheet).

79. Taufschein.
    Imprint: Allentown; Gedruckt und zu haben bey Henrich Ebner, 1820.
    Woodcut with letterpress, on laid paper; 40 × 33 cm (sheet).

80. Taufschein: Catharina Elizabetha Zimmerman.
    Imprint: Gedruckt und zu haben von Jacob Baab, Frontstrasse. Harrisburg.
    ca. 1827.
    Woodcut with letterpress and watercolor, on wove paper; 41 × 32 cm (sheet).

81. Taufschein: Joel Boyer.
    Imprint: Reading, Pa. Gedruckt und zu haben bey Johann Ritter und comp.
    1848.
    Woodcut with letterpress, on wove paper; 42.5 × 33.5 cm (sheet).

82. Taufschein: Clarra Resch.
    Imprint: Reading, Pa. Gedruckt und zu haben bey Ritter u. co.
    1870.
    Woodcut with letterpress, on wove paper; 43 × 34 cm (sheet).

83. Taufschein: William Zacharias Weiandt.
    Imprint: Gedruckt und zu haben an dem "Eagle" Buchstohr. 542 Penn Strasse, Reading, Pa.
    ca. 1877.
    Woodcut with letterpress and watercolor, on wove paper; 43 × 35 cm (sheet).

84. Baptismal Certificate: Mary Caine.
    Imprint: Printed and For Sale At The "Eagle" Book Store, No. 542 Penn Street, Reading, Pa.
    1871.
    Woodcut with letterpress and watercolor, on wove paper; 43 × 33.5 cm (sheet).

    English version of entry 83.

85. Baptismal Certificate: Olive Grace Stoyer.
    Imprint: Printed and For Sale At The "Eagle" Book Store, No. 542 Penn Street, Reading, Pa.
    1902.
    Woodcut with letterpress and watercolor, on wove paper; 43.5 × 35.5 cm (sheet).

86. Baptismal Certificate: Charles Walter Dankel.
    Imprint: Printed and For Sale At The "Eagle" Book Store, No. 542 Penn Street, Reading, Pa.
    1881.
    Woodcut with letterpress and watercolor, on wove paper; 43 × 35.5 cm (sheet).

87. Taufschein.
    Imprint: Reading, Pa. Gedruckt und zu haben bey Carl Kessler.
    Woodcut with letterpress and watercolor, on wove paper; 41 × 33 cm (sheet).

    Blank certificate.

88. Taufschein: Daniel Gottschall.
    ca. 1813.
    Woodcut with letterpress and watercolor, on wove paper; 39.5 × 30.5 cm (sheet).
    LC-USZ62-93919

89. Taufschein: Thomas Monro Zettelmayer.
    Imprint: Gedruckt und zu haben bey G. S. Peters, Harrisburg, Pa.
    ca. 1840.
    Woodcut with letterpress, on wove paper; 41 × 33 cm (sheet).
    LC-USZ62-93927

90. Taufschein: Theyna Chapel.
    Imprint: Gedruckt und zu haben bey H.W. Villee, In der Nordlichen Quien Strasse, in Lancaster, (Pa.) . . .
    ca. 1830.
    Woodcut with letterpress, on wove paper; 41 × 33 cm (sheet).
    LC-USZ62-93924

91. Taufschein: Maria Steiner.
    Unidentified artist.
    between 1800 and 1823.
    Woodcut with letterpress and watercolor, on laid paper; 33 × 40.5 cm (sheet).
    LC-USZ62-93928

92. Taufschein: George Hofman.
    Imprint: Gezeichnet und gestochen von C.F. Egelmann.
    1812.
    Engraving with stipple, on laid paper; 31 × 25 cm (plate) and 33 × 29 cm (sheet).

93. Taufschein: Susanna Umbehend.
    Imprint: Gezeichnet und gestochen von C.F. Egelmann.
    1793.
    Engraving with stipple, on laid paper: 29.5 × 25 cm (sheet).

94. Taufschein: William Leiby.
    Signed: M.H. Traubel.
    Imprint: Zu haben bei C. L. Rademacher, 39 Nord Vierte Str. Swischer, Arch & Cherry, Philadelphia.
    1849.
    Woodcut with letterpress and watercolor, on wove paper; 41.5 × 30.5 cm (sheet).

Item 91. Birth and baptismal certificate for Maria Steiner, b. 1800.

95. Taufschein.
    Signed: H. Sebald.
    Imprint: Zu Verfassen bei Ir. Kohler, No. 104 Nord Bierte Strass, Philadelphia.
    Woodcut with letterpress and watercolor, on wove paper; 38.5 × 27 cm (sheet).

    Blank certificate. Bears copyright imprint: Entered . . . 1855 by I.G. Kohler . . . Pa.

96. Baptismal Certificate.
    Signed: H. Sebald.
    Imprint: For Sale by Ig. Kohler, No. 104 North 4th St., Philadelphia.
    Woodcut with letterpress and watercolor, on wove paper; 38 × 27 cm (sheet).

    Blank certificate. Bears copyright imprint: Entered . . . 1855 by Ig. Kohler . . . Pa.

97. Taufschein: Samuel Trump.
Signed: Hugo Sebald.
1842.
Woodcut with letterpress and watercolor, on laid paper; 34.5 × 25 cm (sheet).

98. Taufschein: Emma Luisy Weiandt.
Signed: Hugo Sebald.
Imprint: Verlag bey Ig. Kohler, 202 N. 4te Strasse, Philadelphia.
1867.
Color woodcut with letterpress, on wove paper; 34 × 26 cm (sheet).
LC-USZ62-93924

99. Taufschein: John Wilson Weiandt.
Imprint: Gedruckt und zu haben bei Th. F. Scheffer, Harrisburg.
1869.
Color woodcut with letterpress, on wove paper; 42 × 33.5 cm.

100. Baptismal Certificate.
Imprint: Printed and for Sale by Theo. F. Scheffer, Harrisburg, Penna.
1869.
Color woodcut with letterpress, on wove paper; 43 × 32.5 cm (sheet).

Blank certificate.

101. Taufschein: Retosi Werthman.
Imprint: Gedruckt und zu haben bei Lutz & Scheffer, Harrisburg.
1836.
Color woodcut with letterpress, on wove paper; 41 × 32 cm (sheet).

102. Taufschein: Susana Rudy.
Imprint: Gedruckt und zu haben bei Lutz & Scheffer, Harrisburg.
1853.
Color woodcut with letterpress, on wove paper; 42 × 33 cm (sheet).

103. Taufschein: Heinrich Ruthÿ.
Imprint: Gedruckt und zu haben bei Lutz & Scheffer, Harrisburg.
1848.
Color woodcut with letterpress, on wove paper; 42 × 33 cm (sheet).

104. Taufschein.
Imprint: Published by Schafer & Koradi, S.W. 4th & Wood Sts., Philadelphia.
Lithograph with watercolor, on wove paper; 41 × 32 cm (sheet).

Certificate is partially inscribed but the names are illegible.

105. Taufschein: Valentin Miller.
Imprint: Gedruckt und zum Verkauf bei Leisenring, Trexler und Co., "Welte-Bote"—Allentown, Pa.
1873.
Woodcut with letterpress, on wove paper; 43 × 35.5 cm (sheet).

106. Baptismal Certificate with calligraphic drawing by hand: Samuel Sheets.
Imprint: A.E. Synder, Printer, Pottsville, Pa.
L. Johnson & Co.
1865.
Wood engraving, printed in blue ink, on wove paper; 38 × 26.5 cm (sheet).

Calligraphy done in brown ink.

107. Adam and Eve in Paradise.
Imprint: Gedruckt bey Samuel Bauman (Penn).
Woodcut with letterpress and watercolor, on laid paper; 40.5 × 33.5 cm (sheet).

The phrase "Mel. Herzlich thut mich verlangen" appears above the image. It translates "Melody. In my heart, I am longing for you."

108. Adam and Eve in Paradise.
Unidentified artist.
Woodcut with letterpress and watercolor, on wove paper; 34.5 × 31cm (sheet).

"Mel. Herzlich thuth mich Verlangen" appears above image. See entry 107 for translation.

109. Adam und Eva, im Paradies.
Imprint: Reading, Pa. Gedruckt bei C. Bruckman.
Woodcut with letterpress and watercolor, on wove paper; 40.5 × 31.5 cm (sheet).

"Mel. Herzlich thut mich verlangen" appears above image. See entry 107 for translation.
LC-USZ62-58623.

110. Adam und Eva, im Paradies.
    Imprint: Reading, Pa., gedruckt bey C.A. Bruckman.
    Woodcut with letterpress and watercolor, on laid paper; 41 × 31 cm (sheet).

    "Mel. Herzlich thrut mich verlangen" appears above image. See entry 107 for translation.
    LC-USZ62-93923
    LC-USZC4-1218

111. Adam und Eva, im Paradies.
    Imprint: Reading, gedruckt bey C. A. Bruckman.
    Woodcut with letterpress and watercolor, on wove paper; 35 × 28.5 cm (sheet).

    "Mel. Herzlich thut mich verlangen" appears above image. See entry 107 for translation.

112. Adam und Eva im Paradies.
    Imprint: Reading, Gedruckt u. zu haben bey Meyers und Christian.
    Woodcut with letterpress and watercolor, on laid paper; 41 × 33 cm (sheet).

    "Mel. Herzlich thut mich verlangen" appears above image. See entry 107 for translation.

113. Adam und Eva im Paradies.
    Imprint: Reading, Gedruckt und zu haben bey David Roths.
    Woodcut with letterpress and watercolor, on laid paper; 39 × 29 cm (sheet).

    "Mel. Herzlich thut mich verlangen" appears above image. See entry 107 for translation.

114. Adam und Eva im Paradies.
    Imprint: Reading, Gedruckt und zu haben bey Samuel Meyers.
    Woodcut with letterpress and watercolor, on laid paper; 41 × 33.5 cm (sheet).

    "Mel. Herzlich thut mich verlangen" appears above image. See entry 107 for translation.

115. Adam und Eva im Paradies.
    Unidentified artist.
    Woodcut with letterpress and watercolor, on laid paper; 34.5 × 31 cm (sheet).

    "Mel. Herzlich thut mich verlangen" appears above image. See entry 107 for translation.

116. A Metamorphosis drawing in four parts.
    Unidentified artist.
    1841.
    Pencil, watercolor and ink, on ruled, wove paper; 29.5 × 39 cm (sheet, open).

    Lines of verse begin: Adam comes first upon the stage / And Eve from out his side / . . ."

117. Historie von Joseph und seinen Brüdern. [History of Joseph and his Brothers]
    Imprint: Harrisburg, Pa. Gedruckt und zu haben bey G.S. Peters, 1832.
    Woodcut with letterpress and watercolor, on laid paper; 48.5 × 40 cm (sheet).
    LC-USZ62-58617

118. Die Geburt Christi. [The Birth of Christ]
    Imprint: Gedruckt und zu haben bey G. S. Peters, Harrisburg, Pa.
    Woodcut with letterpress and stencil coloring, on wove paper; 35.5 × 25.5 cm (sheet).

    See entry 6 for duplicate print.

119. Der Einzug Christi in Jerusalem. [The Entry of Christ into Jerusalem]
    Imprint: Gedruckt und zu haben bey G.S. Peters, Harrisburg, Pa.
    Woodcut with letterpress and stencil coloring, on laid paper; 36.5 × 25 cm (sheet).

    See entry 7 for duplicate print.

120. The Lord's Supper. Das Heilige Abendmahl.
    Imprint: Printed & For Sale by G.S. Peters, Harrisburg, Pa.
    Woodcut with letterpress and stencil coloring, on wove paper; 35 × 25.5 cm (sheet).

121. Das ungerechte Gericht. [The Unjust Court]
    Imprint: Gedruckt und zu haben bey G.S. Peters, Harrisburg.
    Woodcut with letterpress and stencil coloring, on wove paper; 25.5 × 36.5 cm (sheet).
    LC-USZ62-58620

122. Das ungerechte Gericht. [The Unjust Court]
    Imprint: Gedruckt und zu haben bey G.S. Peters, Harrisburg.
    Woodcut with letterpress and stencil coloring, on wove paper; 25.5 × 36.5 cm (sheet).

    See entry 121 for duplicate print with different coloring.

Item 127. Gabriel Miesse (1807–1886), artist. House blessing.

Item 132. Gustave Sigismund Peters (1793–1847), artist. Print, G. S. Peters.

123. Die Kreuzigung Christi.
    [The Crucifixion of Christ]
    Signed: Henry Sc.
    Imprint: Gedruckt und zu haben bey H.B. Villee.
    Woodcut with letterpress, on wove paper; 38.5 × 30 cm (sheet).

124. Bis in des alters Tagen will er mich.
    Unidentified artist.
    1828.
    Pen and ink, watercolor, and gouache, on wove paper; 25.5 × 34 cm (sheet).

125. Haus-Segen.
    Unidentified artist.
    ca. 1800.
    Woodcut with letterpress, on laid paper; 33 × 36.5 cm (sheet).

    See entry 126 for duplicate print.
    LC-USZ62-3142

126. Haus-Segen.
    Unidentified artist.
    ca. 1800.
    Woodcut with letterpress, on laid paper; 32 × 40 cm (sheet).

    See entry 125 for duplicate print.

127. Haus-Segen.
    Signed: G. Miesse SC.
    Woodcut with letterpress and watercolor, on wove paper; 40.5 × 33.5 cm (sheet).
    LC-USZ62-93926

128. Haus-Segen.
    Unidentified artist.
    Woodcut with letterpress, on wove paper; 32.5 × 40 cm (sheet).

129. Haus-Segan.
    Imprint: Reading, gedruckt und zu haben bey Johann Ritter und Comp.
    Woodcut with letterpress and watercolor, on wove paper; 41 × 32.5 cm (sheet).
    LC-USZ62-4865

130. Haus-Segen.
    Imprint: Allentaun, [Penna.] Gedruckt und zu haben bei Graeter und Blumer.
    Woodcut with letterpress, watercolor and gouache, on wove paper; 39.5 × 32 cm (sheet).
    LC-USZ62-93914
    LC-USZC4-1214

131. Traue —Schaue —Wem?
    [Trust —Show —To Whom?]
    Imprint: Gedruckt und zu haben bey G.S. Peters, Harrisburg, Pa.
    Woodcut with letterpress and watercolor, on wove paper; 40 × 33.5 cm (sheet).
    LC-USZ62-58618

132. Traue —Schaue —Wem?
    [Trust —Show —To Whom?]
    Imprint: Gedruckt und zu haben bey G.S. Peters, Harrisburg, Pa.
    Woodcut with letterpress, on wove paper; 40.5 × 33 cm (sheet).
    LC-USZ62-93925

133. Ein neues Lied, von der Mordgeschichte des Joseph Miller. [A new song, of the murder story of Joseph Miller]
    Unidentified artist.
    Woodcut wirh letterpress, on wove paper; 45 × 18 cm (sheet).

134. Ein neues Trauer-Lied . . . Susanna Cox . . .
    [A new lament . . . of Susanna Cox]
    Unidentified artist.
    Woodcut with letterpress, on wove paper; 45.5 × 18 cm (sheet).
    LC-USZ62-93911

135. Concordia.
    Unidentified artist.
    Woodcut with letterpress, on wove paper; 38 × 24 cm (sheet).

    Complete title is unknown because portion of paper is missing.
    LC-USZ62-58624

136. Das Neue Jerusalem. [The New Jerusalem]
 Unidentified artist.
 Woodcut with watercolor and letterpress, on wove paper; 31 × 40.5 cm (sheet).
 LC-USZ62-58622

137. New Jerusalem.
 Imprint: Printed and for sale by J.G. Struphar, Annville, Pa. Copyright 1924 by J.G. Struphar.
 Woodcut with letterpress and stencil coloring, on wove paper; 29 × 38 cm.

138. Adam und Eva, im Paradies.
 Imprint: Reading, gedruckt bey C.A. Bruckman.
 Woodcut with letterpress and watercolor, on laid paper; 41 × 33 cm (sheet).

 "Mel. Herzlich thut mich Verlangen" appears above image. See entry 107 for translation.

139. Prayer: Vereinigung der Kinder im Gebet. [Union of the Children Prayer]
 Imprint: Joseph Schnee, Drukter.
 Woodcut with letterpress and watercolor, on laid paper; 16 × 29 cm (sheet).
 LC-USZ62-4863

140. Das glückselige kind. [The Blissful Child]
 Unidentified artist.
 Woodcut with letterpress, on yellow, wove paper; 31 × 25.5 cm (sheet).

141. Himmels-Brief. [Heavenly Letter]
 Unidentified artist.
 Woodcut with letterpress, on wove paper; 45.5 × 34.5 cm (sheet).

142. Himmels-Brief. [Heavenly Letter]
 Unidentified artist.
 Woodcut with letterpress, on wove paper; 43 × 31 cm (sheet).

143. Himmels-Brief. [Heavenly Letter]
 Unidentified artist.
 Woodcut with letterpress, on wove paper: 41 × 30 cm (sheet).

144. Himmels-Brief. [Heavenly Letter]
 Unidentified artist.
 Woodcut with letterpress and watercolor, on wove paper; 37 × 32 cm (sheet).

145. A letter Written by God himself and left down at Magdeburg . . . in the year 1783.
 Imprint: Eagle Job Print, 542 Penn Street, Reading, Pa.
 Woodcut with letterpress, on wove paper; 40 × 26.5 cm (sheet).

 Four German versions of "A letter . . ." follow this one in English. The text warns of working on the Sabbath and carries a warning from God to obey his orders.

146. Ein Brief so von Gott Selbsten geschrieben . . . im Jahre 1783.
 Imprint: Gedruckt bei King & Baird, No. 9 Sansomstrasse, Philadelphia.
 Woodcut with letterpress, on wove paper; 42 × 33 cm (sheet).

 See entry 145.

147. Ein Brief . . . im Jahre 1783.
 Imprint: Gedruckt bei J. Rohr, 345 . . . Strasse, Philadelphia, Pa.
 Woodcut with letterpress, on laid paper; 39.5 × 29 cm (sheet).

 See entry 145.

148. Ein Brief . . . im Jahre 1783.
 Imprint: Gedruckt bei King & Baird, No. 9 Sansomstrasse, Philadelphia.
 Woodcut with letterpress, on laid paper; 40 × 30 cm (sheet).

 See entry 145.

149. Ein Brief . . . im Jahre 1783.
 Imprint: Gedruckt bei Jessee G. Hawley, 542 Penn Strasse, Reading, Pa.
 Woodcut with letterpress and watercolor, on green, laid paper; 41.5 × 27 cm (sheet).

 See note for entry 145.

150. Ich sahe ein Lamm stehen oben auf dem Berge Zion. [I saw a lamb on Mt. Zion]
 Unidentified artist.
 Woodcut with letterpress and watercolor, on wove paper; 43 × 42 cm (sheet).

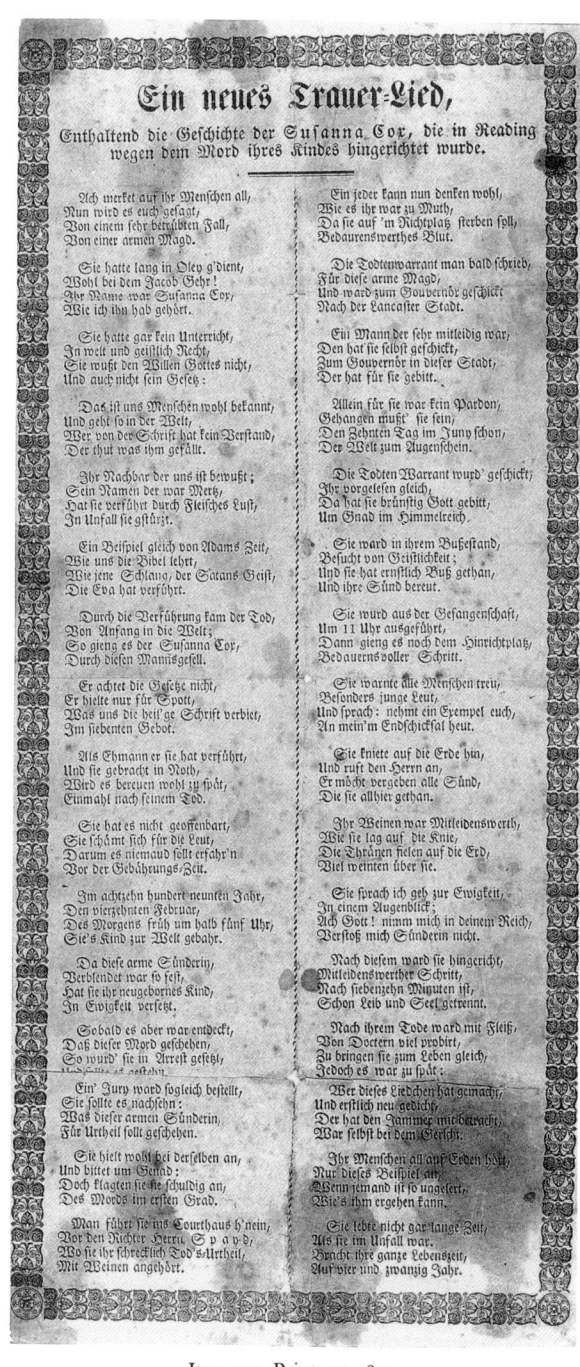

Item 134. Print, ca. 1850.

151. Christlicher Stundenweiser.
 [Christian Hour Guide]
 Imprint: Zu finden in Zug.
 Woodcut with letterpress and watercolor, on laid paper; 40.5 × 33.5 cm (sheet).
 LC-USZ62-4866

152. Geistlicher Irrgarten. [Spritual Labyrinth]
 Imprint: Gedruckt bey G.S. Peters, —Harrisburg, Pa. ca. 1830.
 Woodcut with letterpress, on wove paper; 42 × 31.5 cm (sheet).
 LC-USZ62-58619

153. Das Leben und Alter der Menschen.
 [The Life and Ages of Mankind]
 Imprint: Carlisle, Pa., Gedruckt und zu haben bey Moser und Peters, 1826.
 Woodcut with letterpress, on wove paper; 33 × 39.5 cm (sheet).
 LC-USZ62-93913

154. Die zwei Bruder und Zwillinge Romus und Remulus . . . [The two twin brothers, Romulus and Remus . . .]
 Unidentified artist.
 Wash, pen and ink, and watercolor, on laid paper; 33 × 39.5 cm (sheet).

155. Galloping horse.
 Unidentified artist.
 Pen and brown ink, on laid paper; 20 × 31.5 cm (sheet).

156. Trotting horse.
 Signed: Daniel Hartz 1870.
 Pencil on laid paper; 20 × 33.5 cm (sheet).

157. Leaping horse.
 Unidentified artist.
 Pencil, pen and brown ink with watercolor, on wove paper; 20.5 × 31 cm (sheet).

Index of Names

Adam, Ann Elizabeth, 64
Adam, Jacob, 64
Adam, Heinrich, 64

Beissel, Johann Conrad, Performing Arts, 39
Blossin, Henrich, 55
Blossin, Magdalena, 55
Blossin, Salome Peter Handwerk, 55
Blumin, Daniel, 56
Blümin, Maria, 57
Blümin, Peter, 57
Blumin, Sussanna, 56
Blunt, William, 46
Boyer, Catharina Adam, 81
Boyer, Heinrich, 81
Boyer, Joel, 81
Brant, Samuel, Rare Book

Caine, Henry, 84
Caine, Mary (mother), 84
Caine, Mary (daughter), 84
Chapel, Ehster Millern, 90
Chapel, Perimins, 90
Chapel, Theyna, 90
Cox, Susanna, 134

Dankel, Charles Walter, 86
Dankel, Levi, 86
Dankel, Mary Kurr, 86

Engelmann, Carl Friedrich, Rare Book

Felix, Anthony, 73
Felix, Catarina Martarin, 73
Furnald, Mary, 46

Gottschall, Anna Maria Kessler, 88
Gottschall, Daniel, 88
Gottschall, Jacob, 88

Heilman, Adam, 53
Heilman, Catharina (mother), 53
Heilman, Catharina (daughter), 53
Heinle, David, 69
Heinle, Johanne, 69
Heinle, Magdalena Dimnerin, 69
Henrich, Georg, 68
Henrich, Johanes, 68
Henrich, Rosina Arnerin, 68
Hofman, Elizabeth Schazbell, 92
Hofman, George, 92
Hofman, Michael, 92

Keller, Catharina Ohlinger, 71
Keller, Johannes, 71
Keller, Peter, 71
Kinnig, Catharina, 8
Kraemer, Abraham, 65
Kraemer, Catharina Nosser, 65
Kraemer, Magdalena, 65

Leiby, Eva Niefert, 94
Leiby, Jacob, 94
Leiby, William, 94

Meily, Jacob, Jenks 1
Meily, Johannes, Jenks 1
Meily, Veronica, Jenks 1
Miller, Elisabeth Schaefer, 72
Miller, Enoch, 72
Miller, Isaac, 105
Miller, Jonathan, 72
Miller, Joseph, 133
Miller, Rebecca Zettlemeyer, 105
Miller, Valentin, 105

Neu, Heinrich, 61
Neu, Maria Losslin, 61
Neu, Sally, 61
Noll, Susana, 76

Peter, Esther, 1
Peter, Maria Merckelin, 1
Peter, Michael, 1
Purman, Catharina Greinerin, 70
Purman, Johannes, 70
Purman, Joseph, 70

Resch, Clarra, 82
Resch, Henri, 82
Resch, Meside Potteiger, 82
Rothermel, Elisabeth Miller, 74
Rothermel, Johannes, 74
Rothermel, Leonhardt, 74
Rudy, Catharina Eisenhauer, 63
Rudy, Heinrich (father), 102
Rudy, Jacob, 63
Rudy, Michael, 63
Rudy, Susana, 102
Ruthy, Catharina Batdorff, 102, 103
Ruthÿ, Heinrich (father), 103
Ruthÿ, Heinrich (son), 103

Schall, Jacob, 54
Schall, Johan Peter, 54
Schall, Susanna Frantzin, 54
Schwarin, Adam, 60
Schwarin, Anna Barbara, 60
Schwarin, Anna Christina Gyrerin, 60
Schwartz, Elisabeth Hessin, 66
Schwartz, Johannes, 66
Schwartz, Samuel, 66
Shadt, Johan Wendel, 58
Sheets, Jared, 106
Sheets, Mary Moyer, 106
Sheets, Samuel, 106
Staut, Elizabeth, 62
Staut, Jacob, 62
Staut, Wilhelm, 63
Steiger, Catharina Weitman, 78

Steiger, Samuel, F., 78
Steiger, Semial Hermann, 78
Stein, Anna Maria Steberin, 67
Stein, Henrich, 67
Stein, Philip, 67
Steiner, Lietia Rieten, 91
Steiner, Maria, 91
Steiner, Michael, 91
Stiely, Catharina Wilmeyer, 77
Stiely, Maria Magdalena, 77
Stiely, Phillip, 77
Stoyer, Clara Resh, 85
Stoyer, Olive Grace, 85
Stoyer, Samuel, H., 85

Trump, Christina, 97
Trump, Josiah, 97
Trump, Samuel, 97

Weiandt, Anna Leibesberger, 83, 98, 99
Weiandt, Emma Luisy, 98
Weiandt, John, 83, 98, 99
Weiandt, John Wilson, 99
Weiandt, William Zacharias, 83
Wenrich, Catharin Umbenhaurer, 75
Wenrich, Salome, 75
Wenrich, Thomas, 75
Werthman, Retosi, 101
Werthman, Rebecca Trautmann, 101
Werthman, Samuel, 101
Whitemore, Matilda, 33

Zettlemayer, Christina Eisenhauer, 89
Zettlemayer, Martin, 89
Zettlemayer, Thomas Monro, 89
Zimmerman, Catharina Elizabetha, 79
Zimmerman, Elizabetha Gererich, 79
Zimmerman, Jacob, 79

Index of Artists and Publishers

Baab, Jacob, 80
Bauman, Samuel, 63, 107
Brechall, Martin, 54
Bruckman, C., 109–11

Dell, R. A., 41

Eagle Job Print, 145
Egelmann, C. F., 92, 93

Gregg, Sarah, 24

Hartz, Daniel, 157
Hawley, Jesse G., 149
Henry, 123

Johnson, L. & Co., 106
Jungman, Gottlob, 64

Kessler, Carl, 87
King & Baird, 146, 148
Kinnig, Catharina, 8
Koumin, Margreta, 3
Krebs, Friederich, 60, 65–69
Kundig, Samuel, 9

Leisenring, Trexler & Co., 105
Lepper, Wilhelm, 58
Lutz & Scheffer, 101–3

Menz, George W., 61
Meyers & Christian, 112
Meyers, Samuel, 114
Meylon, Johannes, Jenks 1, 2
Miesse, G., 127

Peters, G. S., 6, 7, 89, 117–22, 131, 132, 152

Rank, William, 26, 27
Rassmann, Henrich, Jenks 4–6
Rieshe, W., 52
Ritter, Johan, 71–79, 81–86, 129
Rohr, J., 147
Roth, Daniel, 113

Schaefer & Korade, 104
Scheffer, Theodore F., 99, 100
Schnee, Joseph, 139
Sebald, H., 95–98
Stover, J., 59
Struphar, J. G., 137

Traubel, M. H., 94

Umbehend, Susanna, 93

Villee, H. V., 90, 123

Weigner, Sarah, 44
Whitemore, Ruth, 33
Wiestling, John S., 70
Wright, Penrose, 45

45

Selected Bibliography

Abrahams, Ethel Ewert. *Frakturmalen und Schönschreiben: The Fraktur Art and Penmanship of the Dutch-German Mennonites while in Europe, 1700–1900.* North Newton, Kansas: Mennonite Press, Inc., 1980.
ND3125.A27

Borneman, Henry S. *Pennsylvania German Bookplates.* Philadelphia, 1953. Pennsylvania German Society.
F146.P23, v. 54

Borneman, Henry S. *Pennsylvania German Illuminated Manuscripts.* Norristown, 1937. Pennsylvania German Society.
v. 46 (NOS)

Calligraphy & Handwriting in America, 1710–1962. Assembled and Shown by the Peabody Institute Library, Baltimore, Maryland, November, 1961–January, 1962. Caledonia, New York: Italimuse, Inc., 1963.
Z43.P37

Dewhurst, C. Kurt. Betty MacDowell and Marsha MacDowell. *Religious Folk Art in America: Reflections of Faith.* New York: E. P. Dutton, Inc., in association with the Museum of American Folk Art, 1983.
NK805.D49, 1983

Fabian, Monroe H. "The Easton Bible Artist Identified." *Pennsylvania Folklife,* XXII:2 (Winter 1972–73), 2–14.

Garvan, Beatrice B. *The Pennsylvania German Collection.* Philadelphia: Philadelphia Museum of Art, 1982.
NK835.P4P5, 1982

Garvan, Beatrice B. and Charles F. Hummel. *The Pennsylvania Germans: A Celebration of Their Arts, 1683–1850.* Philadelphia: Philadelphia Museum of Art, 1982.
NK835.P4P53

Hollyday, Guy Tilghman. "The Ephrata Codex: Relationships Between Text and Illustration." *Pennsylvania Folklife,* XX:1 (Autumn 1970), 28–43.

Hollyday, Guy Tilghman. "The Ephrata Wall-Charts and Their Inscriptions." *Pennsylvania Folklife,* XIX:3 (Spring 1970), 34–46.

Hopf, Carroll. "Calligraphic Drawings and Pennsylvania German Fraktur." *Pennsylvania Folklife,* XXII:1 (Autumn 1972), 2–9.

Leeds, Wendy. "Fraktur: An Annotated Bibliography." *Pennsylvania Folklife,* XXV:4 (Summer 1976), 35–46.

Lichten, Frances. *Folk Art of Rural Pennsylvania.* New York: Charles Scribner's Sons, 1946.
NK835.P4L5

Mercer, Henry C. "The Survival of the Mediaeval Art of Illuminative Writing Among Pennsylvania Germans." *Proceedings of the American Philosophical Society,* XXXVI: 156 (December 1897), pp. 424–33.
F157.B8.B86

Morse, John D., editor. *Prints in and of America to 1850.* Charlottesville, Virginia: Published for The Henry Francis DuPont Winterthur Museum by the University Press of Virginia, 1970.

Patterson, Daniel W. *Gift Drawing and Gift Song: A Study of Two Forms of Shaker Inspiration*. Sabbathday Lake, Maine: The United Society of Shakers, 1983.

Shelly, Donald A. *The Fraktur-Writings of Illuminated Manuscripts of the Pennsylvania Germans*. Allentown, 1961. Pennsylvania German Folklore Society, Volume XXIII (1958–59).
GR110.P4A35, V. 23

Shoemaker, Alfred L. *Check List of Pennsylvania Dutch Printed Taufscheins*. Lancaster: Pennsylvania Dutch Folklore Center, 1952.

Stoudt, John Joseph. *Consider the Lilies, How They Grow: An Interpretation of the Symbolism of Pennsylvania German Art*. Pennsylvania German Folklore Society, Volume II (1937). Revised edition: *Pennsylvania Folk-Art: An Interpretation*. Allentown, Pennsylvania: Schlechter's, 1948.

Stoudt, John Joseph. *Early Pennsylvania Arts and Crafts*. New York: A. S. Barnes and Co., Inc., 1964.
NK835.P4S72

Swank, Scott T. et al. *Arts of the Pennsylvania Germans*. New York: Published for The Henry Francis DuPont Winterthur Museum by W. W. Norton & Co., 1983.
N6530.P458 1983

Weiser, Frederick S. "Piety and Protocol in Folk Art: Pennsylvania German Fraktur Birth and Baptismal Certificates." *Winterthur Portfolio*, VIII (1973), 19–43.

Weiser, Frederick S. and J. Howell Heaney, compilers. *The Pennsylvania German Fraktur of The Free Library of Philadelphia: An Illustrated Catalogue*. 2 volumes. Breinigsville, Pennsylvania: The Pennsylvania German Society and The Free Library of Philadelphia, 1976. Publications of the Pennsylvania German Society, Volume X (1976).
ND3035.P4W44

Wust, Klaus. *Virginia Fraktur: Penmanship as Folk Art*. Edinburg, Virginia: Shenandoah History, 1972.
ND3035.V8W8

Yoder, Don. "The Country Printer and the Taufschein." *The Second Lancaster Heritage Antique Show 1973*. Lancaster: Farm & Home Foundation, 1973, pp. 4–13.

Yoder, Don. "Fraktur in Mennonite Culture." *The Mennonite Quarterly Review*, pp. 305–42.
BX8101.M4 v. ?

Yoder, Don, Vernon S. Gunnion, and Carroll J. Hopf. *Pennsylvania German Fraktur and Color Drawings*. Lancaster: Pennsylvania Farm Museum of Landis Valley, 1969.

The text of this book was set in Galliard by Graphic Composition, Athens, Georgia, with display type set in Fraktur by Phils Photo, Washington, D.C. The cover paper is King James Cast Coat, and the text paper is Dulcet Text, Smooth Finish. The book was designed by John Crank & Associates and printed in an edition of 2,500 copies by Whittet & Shepperson Printers, Richmond, Virginia.